An Expert Guide to
PROBLEM SOLVING
With Practical Examples

ADITI AGARWAL

To Shri Shirdi Sai Ram

To my son, Aryan, for inspiring me

To my husband, Krishan, for his loving support

To my mom & dad, for always standing by me

Table of Contents

Preface 5
Acknowledgements..7
Chapter 1 – Rationale..8
Chapter 2 – What Is Fishbone Diagram?.........12
Chapter 3 – Fishbone Examples.......................24
Chapter 4 – What Is Brainstorming? 34
Chapter 5 – Brainstorming Examples 42
Chapter 6 – What Is SWOT?...........................46
Chapter 7 – SWOT Examples..........................52
Chapter 8 – What Is FMEA Technique?..........56
Chapter 9 - FMEA Examples 66
Chapter 10 – What Is 5Whys Technique? 70
Chapter 11 – 5Whys Examples 73
Chapter 12 – Comparison................................76
Bibliography 81

Preface

Most of us encounter problems in our lives, either at work or at home. These problems cause stress in our minds and leave us exhausted. Instinctively, we start to take ad-hoc actions that we think will resolve the problem, but we soon realize that our actions are not effective and do not prevent or solve the core problem.

In 1940s, Alex Osborn introduced a structured way to problem solving. Since then, several scientists and researchers have contributed to problem solving.

Structured problem solving provides a systematic approach to identifying the root causes to a problem. Many scientific tools and methods have been developed to identify effective solutions to any problem. The most widely used problem solving techniques are Fishbone Diagram, Brainstorming, SWOT, Failure Modes and Effects Analysis, and 5Whys.

Several organizations leverage these problem-solving methods to manage their problems at work. Learning about problem solving tools will help you to effectively solve your problems at work and in everyday life.

There are many types of problems. Problems that have only one correct answer such as math problems, puzzles, test questions, quizzes etc. are outside the scope of this book. On the other hand, problems that have multiple correct answers such as life problems are the ones we will discuss in this book.

This book will give you an understanding of the different problem solving tools along with practical examples and applications of these tools.

Acknowledgements

First and foremost, I would like to express my gratitude to God, whose blessings gave me the courage to write this book.

I would like to thank my husband, Krishan, for his time to review this book and provide valuable feedback.

I would like to give special thanks to my son, Aryan, whose curious questions regarding my work, triggered an idea to write this book.

Chapter 1 – Rationale

"Most of our problems are because we act without thinking or we keep thinking without acting."

The phone rings. It is 10PM. My project developer informs me that our application is failing in production and asks me to join the bridge call. After three hours of intense late night discussion, it was discovered that a recent code deployment by another team caused our application to break!

Likewise, many of us experience problems in our day-today lives. One may find it difficult to take a decision at work, while other may be struggling to keep things in the right order at home.

An architect may be trying to solve for the best technical approach, a manager may be experiencing the problem of having an unmotivated member in the team, a developer might not have the skills to work on the new technology, a person might not be happy with his current job, a parent might be struggling with the behavior of his/her kid, a student might not know how to improve his/her grades, or a person might be thinking the best way to tackle his/her health condition.

Likewise, an organization might not know the most effective method to win the confidence of the customers, a project team might not know the root cause of its' unsuccessful launch, a manager might not understand why the team failed to perform and so on.

If any of this resonates with you, you will agree that most people in this world have problems that they are trying to solve.

Most people tend to follow their instincts when it comes to problem solving. Thus, their actions often do not solve the problem and prove to be in-effective.

Many scientists accepted the need for structured thinking and came up with different techniques for scientific problem solving.

In 1940s, Alex Osborn introduced the technique of “Brainstorming” with his book titled “How To Think Up”. Later in 1960s, Kaoru Ishikawa, who was one of the founding fathers of modern management, popularized the “Ishikawa” or “Fishbone diagram” technique.

The problem-solving techniques provide many benefits to us such as:

- Reduce and eliminate recurring problems
- Improve operational efficiency
- Provide a repeatable approach
- Promote team collaboration
- Enable critical decision making

All of us need to learn problem solving tools and techniques to be able to make informed decisions and take effective actions to solve everyday problems.

In the next few chapters, we will learn about the popular Fishbone diagram, Brainstorming, SWOT, FMEA analysis, and 5Whys techniques.

Chapter 2 – What Is Fishbone Diagram?

"Education is the key to unlock the golden door of freedom."

- *George W. Carver*

Often, in our day to day lives or at work, we encounter problems or roadblocks to proceed further. To solve any problem, we think about the potential causes for the problem and take corrective action. Many a times, there are numerous causes for the problem which makes it difficult for us to identify the most significant causes. It is important to narrow down to the critical few so we can focus our energies and efforts to get rid of them and mitigate the problem.

One of the most commonly used approach to categorize the root causes for a problem is called a Fishbone Diagram. This is also known as a "Cause and Effect Diagram" or an "Ishikawa Diagram". It is also considered as one of the basic tools for quality management. The name "fishbone" comes from the fact that it is shaped like a skeleton of a fish.

Fishbone or Ishikawa diagrams were created in 1968 by Kaoru Ishikawa who was a Japanese Professor at the University of Tokyo and was famous for his inventions for quality management.

The fishbone diagram is being used across several software and manufacturing organizations as a simple visualization tool to depict various potential causes to a problem. It provides a structured way to organize and represent data in a meaningful manner.

The fishbone diagram is a pictorial representation and categorization of possible known causes to a problem, usually gathered during brainstorming. Brainstorming is a creative technique where a group of people come together and generate a list of ideas to solve a problem. You will read about the brainstorming technique later in this book.

You can apply the fishbone diagram method in solving day-to-day problems as well. This technique can be used whenever there are many possible causes to a problem or whenever there is a need to identify causes to a complex problem.

This technique is mostly conducted in a group with people from different fields of expertise. However, this method can also be used by an individual as a tool to structure one's thoughts and identify root causes.

Shape of a Fishbone Diagram:

The below figure (Fig. 1) shows the shape of a typical fishbone diagram:

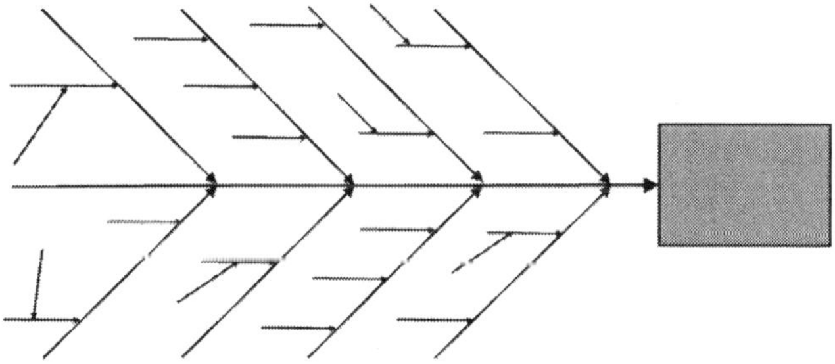

Fig. 1: Shape of a Fishbone Diagram

As you can see, the shape of the above diagram resembles a fish skeleton! Hence, this diagram is popularly known as the Fishbone Diagram.

To create a fishbone diagram, the problem that one is trying to solve is written on the right-hand side within a box or a circle. Next, a central arrow is drawn that connects to the problem box or circle. This is called the 'Main Arrow' (refer to Fig. 2).

Fig. 2: Fishbone - Problem

The major categories for the causes to this problem are written on the branches connecting to the main arrow (refer to Fig. 3).

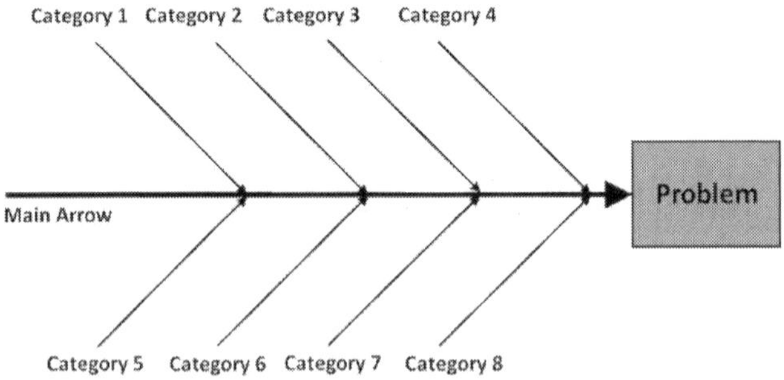

Fig. 3: Fishbone - Categories

Each of the primary causes to the problem are then notated as a branch from the appropriate category. The secondary or the sub-causes branch-off the primary causes and so on (refer to Fig. 4).

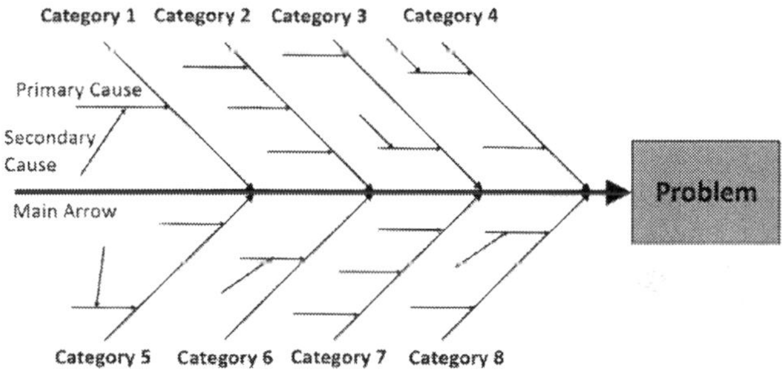

Fig. 4: Fishbone - Primary & Secondary Causes

Categories of a Fishbone Diagram:

The categories or the headings give a direction to our thoughts and help us in identifying primary causes associated with that problem.

Let's take an example problem statement that a person is not able to focus at work. If you were to list down all the causes to this problem, you may not know where to begin. However, if I give you the main categories as ‘People’, ‘Environment’, and ‘Materials’, you will immediately start thinking about the causes that relate to these categories. In this scenario, one of the causes under ‘People’ category could be ‘Poor health of a loved one’ whereas another cause under ‘Environment’ category could be ‘Too much noise’. The major categories, when defined, streamline our thoughts.

The most commonly used categories for identifying the potential causes to a problem are listed as below:

- People
- Methods
- Materials
- Machines
- Measurements
- Environment

The ‘People’ category helps us to identify all causes that are person related. Let’s take an example. One of the leading software organization was having major quality issues and one of the primary causes was the unavailability of skilled resources. When represented on a fishbone diagram, this cause

‘Unavailability of skilled resources’ will appear under the ‘People’ category.

Any causes that deal with the process or method to perform an activity are listed under ‘Methods’ category. Primary causes such as ‘Inefficient development processes’, ‘Unnecessary effort spent by the team’ etc. are few examples of the causes that fit well under the ‘Method’ category.

The ‘Materials’ category is specific to any material or parts required to produce a product. This category is more common in the manufacturing industry. However, within software organizations, this category can be used to group any causes related to external dependencies. For example, if you are making changes to a front-end application that calls a service to fetch some values and if you hit a roadblock, then a primary cause such as ‘Unavailability of the dependent service’ will be represented under this category.

The ‘Machines’ category is used to group all the causes related to hardware, software and tools. For example, one of the primary causes for poor system performance could be the

'Unavailability of additional servers'. Then again, one of the primary causes to ineffective communication within an organization could be the 'Unavailability of collaboration tools'. Such causes are usually grouped under the 'Machines' category on a fishbone diagram.

The 'Measurements' category is used to group the causes that relate to incorrect data to measure the quality or success of the product. Consider an example where your team has launched a new website but the product goal to reduce call volume to the service center is still not met. Now, if one of the primary causes to this problem is the 'Incorrect data gathered during user research of the product', then this primary cause will be represented under the 'Measurements' category on a fishbone diagram.

Causes that relate to an environment are usually grouped under the 'Environments' category. For a manufacturing industry, an example for an environment related cause is 'Lack of appropriate weather conditions or location'. For software organizations, an example of such a cause could be 'Instability of development, test or production environments'.

Though the above categories are the most commonly used categories for a fishbone analysis, people often tend to brainstorm the categories that are relevant to the problem they are trying to solve.

How to conduct a Fishbone in a group?

Let's learn the process to conduct or facilitate a fishbone diagram exercise. First, schedule time to meet with the stakeholders or people who are impacted by the problem and are willing to come together to identify the critical causes to the problem.

Then, you draw a box on the right end of the whiteboard and state the problem inside the box. The intent for this exercise is to brainstorm all the possible causes to this problem and identify the few critical causes that have the highest impact to the problem.

Now, draw a line from left to right that connects to the problem box. This line acts as the 'Spine' of the diagram. Next, you draw the main branches emanating from the spine. These branches represent the main categories to the causes.

You then label each category. Here, you can either leverage the generic categories of People, Methods, Materials, Machines, Measurements and Environment or brainstorm the major categories that are relevant to the specific problem.

Next, you focus on each category and brainstorm all the possible causes to this problem that may fit under that category. Each participant writes a cause on a sticky or post-it card and the facilitator then collects and displays each sticky note as a branch off the category. Sometimes, a cause belongs to more than one category. In such cases, the team mutually agrees the category to which the cause belongs to.

Once the primary causes are identified, the group brainstorms again for sub-causes that relate to the specific primary cause. This exercise continues until the group runs out of ideas.

You have now created a fishbone diagram with the possible causes to the specific problem.

Next, each member of the group must vote for the top three causes that affect the problem the most. The causes that get the maximum votes are then listed as the critical causes to the specific problem.

In this way, the group brainstorms together, identifies the possible causes to the specific problem and then narrows down to the critical few causes.

Chapter 3 – Fishbone Examples

"Opportunity is missed by most people because it is dressed in overalls and looks like work."

– Thomas A. Edison

In this chapter, let us look at some examples for fishbone diagramming technique.

Example 1:

Consider a scenario where a project testing team has reported unusually high number of defects for a software development product.

The project team wants to drill down to the major causes of this problem and take corrective action. They decide to leverage the fishbone diagramming technique as it is one of the most effective problem solving tool.

The team works together, brainstorms all possible primary and secondary causes to the problem, and comes up with the below fishbone diagram (refer to Fig. 5).

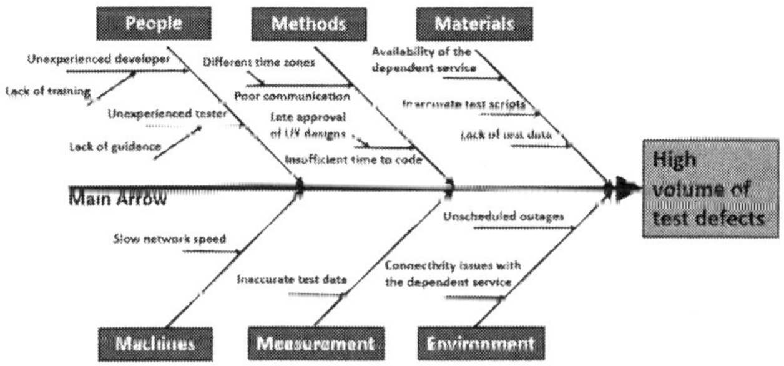

Fig. 5 : Fishbone Diagram for Example1

The team brainstorms and lists the primary causes as below:

- Unexperienced tester
- Unexperienced developer
- Poor communication
- Insufficient time to code
- Unavailability of the dependent service
- Inaccurate test scripts
- Lack of test data
- Unscheduled outages
- Connectivity issues
- Slow network speed
- Inaccurate test data

The team again brainstorms and identifies few secondary causes such as:

- Lack of training
- Lack of guidance
- Different time zones
- Late approval of UX designs

The team then votes for the causes that they think have the most impact to this problem. Consider that the team mutually aligns on the primary causes that led to high volume of defects as below:

- Insufficient time
- Lack of training
- Poor Communication

The team leaders then focus their time and energy on the necessary corrective actions for the above three primary causes to ensure better quality and performance for future projects.

Example 2:

The second example is related to a personal situation where husband and wife are having problems in their married life. They decide to sit together, leverage the fishbone diagramming technique, and brainstorm all the possible causes for their conflicts so they can eliminate the critical few.

The couple aligns on the below important categories to focus their thoughts in the right direction:

- Mutual Understanding
- Language
- Commitment
- Trust
- Ownership

Next, they draw a fishbone diagram and began discussing all the possible causes against each of these categories. Each writes a cause on a sticky note and sticks it to the branch off the relevant category (refer to Fig. 6).

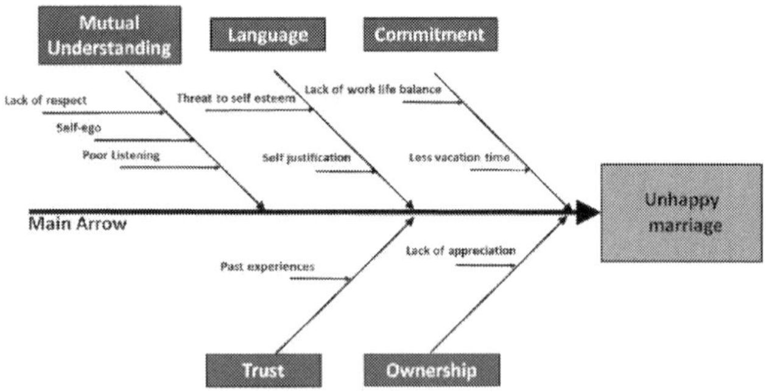

Fig. 6: Fishbone Diagram for Example2

The couple then decides to vote on the ones that are most critical to their situation and aligns that they will focus on showing respect for each other and spending quality time with family.

This exercise not only gave them a platform to collaborate, but also streamlined their thoughts.

Example 3:

Consider another scenario where one is not satisfied with his current job. He wants to change his job, but don't know how. His friends and family understand his problem and want to help. One evening, he invites his friends to his place and decides to use Ishikawa or the Fishbone diagram as a group game to narrow down to critical few causes for the situation.

First, he writes the problem in the rectangular box to the right as "Not able to change job".

Next, he draws the spines with below four widely known categories:

- People
- Materials

- Methods
- Environment

His friends write causes on sticky notes and then stick them to the branch off the relevant category. This exercise continues until the group runs out of ideas.

The group created a fishbone diagram listing all the possible causes to the problem (refer to Fig. 7).

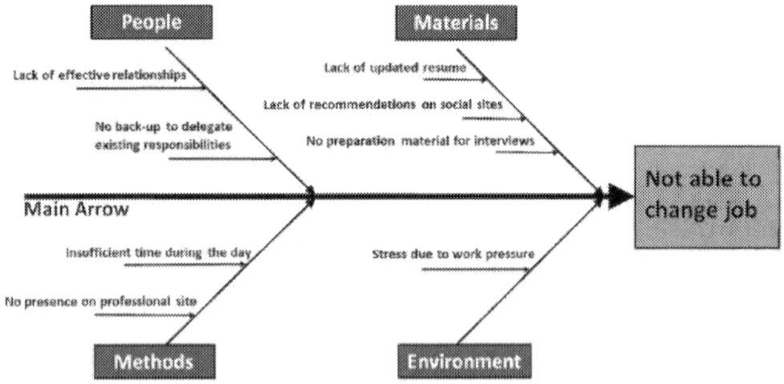

Fig. 7: Fishbone Diagram for Example3

Under the category of 'People', the group identified the below causes:

- Lack of effective relationships (with influencers in other companies)
- No back-up to delegate existing responsibilities

For the category titled 'Materials', the group pins the below causes:

- Lack of updated resume
- Lack of recommendations on social sites
- No preparation material for interviews

Then, under the category of 'Methods', the group listed the below primary causes:

- Insufficient time during the day
- No presence on professional site (LinkedIn)

The group listed below primary cause under the 'Environment' category:

- Stress due to work pressure

The group then voted on the top three causes. Based on all the votes, below causes were shortlisted as the critical ones:

- Lack of updated resume
- No presence on professional site (LinkedIn)
- No back-up to delegate existing responsibilities

This exercise helps him to focus on addressing the critical causes. With diligent efforts in the right direction, he finally gets hired for a new job!

Example 4:

If you are a team leader, you might have experienced the problem of having unmotivated people on the team. If anyone on the team is not motivated to work, it not only affects his own productivity and deliverables, but also negatively impacts others in the team.

In a diverse team, all members of the team have different needs. The motivating factors are not the same.

If you conduct a fishbone diagram with your peers, you will discover a variety of causes contributing to the dis-satisfaction of the team.

I have depicted a simple fishbone diagram here, based on my experience in team management (refer to Fig. 8).

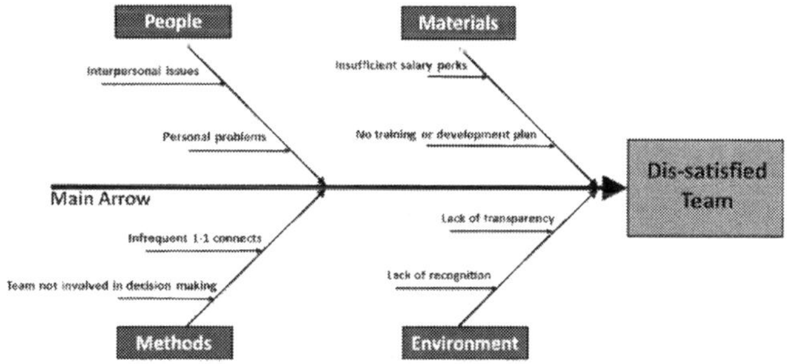

Fig. 8: Fishbone Diagram for Example4

Based on my experience, the top 3 critical causes for a team member to be demotivated are as below:

- Infrequent 1-1 connects
- Lack of recognition
- Insufficient training plan

Chapter 4 – What Is Brainstorming?

"A problem is a chance for you to do your best."

- *Duke Ellington*

Brainstorming is a process to generate creative ideas through group discussion. It is a problem-solving technique where the group generates ideas to solve the problem. In this technique, every participant is encouraged to think and suggest as many ideas as possible. There is no judgement of ideas during this exercise.

In 1940s, Alex F. Osborn began conducting group-thinking sessions to improve the quality and quantity of ideas by employees.

This method was popularized by his book "Applied Imagination" in 1953.

There are four general rules of brainstorming that are listed below:

- Target quantity: The more the number of ideas generated, the better the chances to find a solution.
- Do not criticize: The criticism of ideas generated is put 'On-Hold'. Instead of criticizing the ideas, the participants focus on extending the ideas or creating new ideas.
- Encourage unusual ideas: The unusual ideas are encouraged, promoting 'out of the box' thinking.
- Improve ideas: The participants are encouraged to add to the ideas and generate more ideas.

How to conduct a Brainstorming Session:

There are five steps to conducting an effective brainstorming session as below:

- Prepare the environment: The facilitator or organizer should first create an environment which is comfortable and have all the tools and resources needed to run the session.

  Once the room is ready, a diverse team such as people with different skill sets or thinking styles are invited. The organizer should also appoint one person to record the ideas on sticky notes or the whiteboard.

  All participants should be able to see the sticky notes or ideas always.

- Provide an overview of the problem statement: The organizer presents the problem to the participants along with any historical data or information related to previous attempts to solve the problem.

- Set the schedule and establish rules: The organizer explains the agenda or the schedule of the meeting to the participants. He also communicates the rules for this exercise as below:

- Generate as many ideas as possible
- No idea is bad
- Analysis or judgement of ideas is not allowed until the session ends
- Everyone can build upon other's ideas

- Run the session: The organizer asks all participants to write down their ideas on sticky notes (preferable one idea per sticky note) for first 10-15 minutes.

  Then he asks each participant to share their ideas one by one, while encouraging other participants to build upon the shared idea and create new ideas.

  The organizer stimulates more ideas by asking the participants to perform role based thinking. He also keeps the discussion focused always.

- Organize ideas and act: Towards the end of the brainstorming exercise, the facilitator removes any duplicate or unrelated ideas. The participants then group the ideas into categories or themes.

There are different tools that are available to guide you in organizing and analyzing the ideas such as Affinity Diagrams (a business tool used to organize ideas).

There are many variations for conducting the brainstorming exercise. Two popular variations are freewheeling and round-robin.

In freewheeling approach, participants are encouraged to shout out ideas freely until no one has any more to add. The ideas are written on a white board or flip chart exactly as they are spoken.

In round-robin approach, each member is asked in turn to call out or contribute to an idea, until nobody has anything more to contribute.

Other variations include nominal group technique and directed brainstorming. In nominal group technique, participants write down their ideas anonymously. The facilitator collects all the ideas and the group votes on each idea. The top ranked ideas are then pursued for further discussion.

In directed brainstorming, the participants brainstorm individually and write down their main idea. The written ideas are then shuffled and randomly distributed within the participants. Each participant is asked to improve the written idea and create a new one.

Brainstorming promotes open environment and encourages people to participate and think out of the box or out of their usual ways of thinking. This technique is leveraged not only for problem solving but also to collect feedback and comments from a group.

Some key approaches for Brainstorming:

If the group run short of ideas, there are different approaches that can be used to encourage new ideas:

- Role Playing: In this approach, the participants think from the perspective of another person or role.

  How would a person or role tackle this situation? E.g. in an IT environment, the team may want to think from the viewpoint of their leader, the product sponsor, the compliance officer or the product consumer.

One may also want to create personas for the different types of consumers of the product or service, and think ideas from their perspective.

- Gap Analysis: Another approach to generate more ideas is to write the end goal on the board, identify all the different sub-systems, components or factors that constitute the goal and then encourage the team to think ideas that are focused on these categories and have potential to bridge the gap.

  For example, consider a team whose goal for the brainstorming session is to generate as many ideas as possible to improve the performance of their website by 10%.

  The facilitator or the organizer of the session writes the goal on the board such that it is visible to all the participants.

  Next, he lists down the different sections on the website, different service calls being made to obtain data from the backend databases, business features being rendered on the website etc.

He, then, encourages the participants to think ideas for each of these categories that will help improve the performance of the overall system.

This method helps the participants to think from different angles and focus on reducing the existing gap with their goal.

Interesting Facts about Brainstorming:

- The term was popularized by Alex Faickney Osborn in the 1953 book Applied Imagination.
- This technique is used, not only to generate ideas, but also to collect feedback and comments.
- Brainstorming can also be conducted by a single individual, where one writes down his own ideas.

Chapter 5 – Brainstorming Examples

"The journey of a thousand miles begins with one step."

- Lao Tzu

Brainstorming may be conducted to gather ideas for any problem or goal. Some of the examples are listed below:

- How can we increase the adoption of a website?
- How to reduce the volume of calls made to the customer reps or service call center?

- How to encourage the sales of the product?
- How to minimize the operating expenses?
- How to increase the re-engineering saves?
- How can we encourage the redemption of the loyalty points by the customer?
- How to increase the customer satisfaction?
- How to build strong relationships?

Let's have a practice exercise. Focus on the first problem statement "How can we increase the adoption of a website?" and write down the ideas in the space provided below or on some sticky notes. You may invite your peers or friends and collaborate with them for this exercise or you may just want to pencil down your own thoughts on the given problem. The idea is to practice the art of brainstorming, so you can apply this simple technique in your life.

Next, to organize your ideas, spread out your sticky notes, look for ideas that seem to be related and group them together. Then, the important step is to think a heading for each group.

The below diagram shows a sample grouping of ideas generated from brainstorming for the specified problem statement 'How can we increase the adoption of a website':

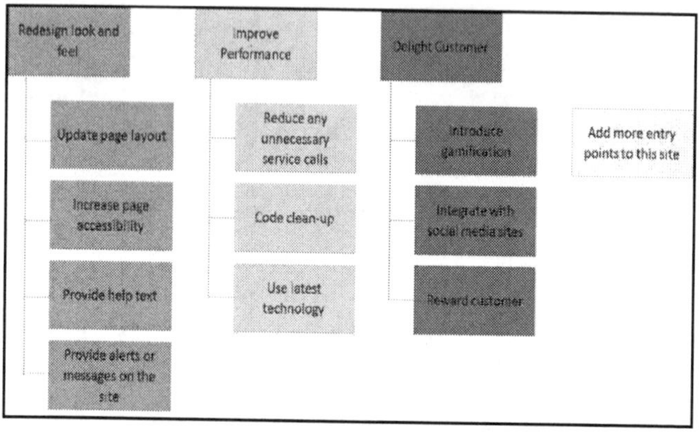

Fig. 9: Sample Affinity Diagram

In the above diagram, as you can see, most of the ideas are categorized into groups, except for one. It is possible that some ideas, being totally unrelated to other ideas, do not fall into any category or group. These groups help organize the generated ideas.

Brainstorming is a very simple and effective technique for solving any problem. It also promotes collaboration between the people and is often leveraged as an ice-breaker or a team building activity.

Chapter 6 – What Is SWOT?

"The measure of who we are is what we do with what we have."

- Vince Lombardi

SWOT analysis (alternatively SWOT matrix) is an acronym for analyzing strengths, weaknesses, opportunities, and threats.

SWOT is a simple, structured and powerful analytical framework for problem solving. Originated by Albert S Humphrey in the 1960s, it helps analyze these four elements for an organization, product, process, service or a person.

SWOT analysis may be used in any decision-making situation when a desired state is known. If an organization needs to take a business decision, create a strategic plan or improve its' existing performance, SWOT analysis is the right choice!

Some of the situations where SWOT analysis is most commonly used are:

- Create organization or personal strategy
- Crisis planning and management
- New business opportunity
- Respond to new trends
- Implement new technology
- New product development
- Increase revenue growth
- Assess competitor strength
- Mitigate resourcing or staffing issues

SWOT Template

SWOT matrix is represented in the form of four quadrants, where each quadrant represents one of four features – strengths, weaknesses, opportunities and threats (as shown in Fig. 10)

Strengths	Weaknesses
Opportunities	Threats

Fig. 10: Template for SWOT Analysis

How to conduct SWOT Analysis:

A SWOT meeting is conducted which allows the participants to creatively brainstorm, and identify strengths, weaknesses, opportunities and threats for an organization, portfolio, project or a given situation.

Strengths are the internal factors that are favorable to an organization, program or project such as culture, expertise, experience, resources etc. It is advisable to think about your strengths from the viewpoint of your competitor as well.

When identifying strengths, one should ask the below questions:

- What advantages do you have over others?
- What is your organization's USP (unique selling propositions)?
- What do others perceive as your strengths?

Weaknesses are the internal factors that that are not favorable for the organization, program or project and should be discussed openly. When thinking about the weaknesses, one should focus on the below questions:

- What factors could be improved?
- What do other perceive as your weakness?
- What makes you lose revenue?

Opportunities are the external factors that are favorable for the organization, program or project such as market trends, weather, environment etc. To identify opportunities, one should ask the following questions:

- What are the opportunities for the project or the organization?
- What are the market trends that you can leverage today?

Threats are external factors or risks that can negatively impact your organization, project, brand or relationships. To list down the possible threats, the below questions should be asked:

- What are the possible risks for the project or organization?
- Is your competitor a threat to you?
- Can any of your listed weaknesses pose a threat to your financial success?

Advantages about SWOT Analysis:

- Simple to understand
- Does not need any statistical knowledge
- Provides quick overview of one's strengths, weaknesses, opportunities and threats
- Useful for strategic planning

Disadvantages about SWOT Analysis:

- SWOT can tend to oversimplify things
- SWOT can result in high number of unmanageable strengths, weaknesses, opportunities & threats.
- SWOT does not enable prioritization.
- People may not find comfortable to discuss some of the weaknesses and threats.

Chapter 7 – SWOT Examples

"Either I will find a way, or I will make one."

- Philip Sidney

In this chapter, let's look at some practical examples for SWOT analysis.

Consider a sample project that takes on this analysis to improve their deliverables (see Fig. 11):

Strengths	Weaknesses
• Highly skilled people • Strong domain knowledge	• Unavailability of working test accounts • Unstable test environments
Opportunities	**Threats**
• Build strong relationship with project sponsor • Deliver a high quality product baseline	• Low business priority • Insufficient Funding • Alignment with external teams

Fig. 11: Sample SWOT for a project

In the above example, while the core strength is availability of highly skilled people with strong domain knowledge, the major weaknesses are unavailability of the working test accounts and unstable test environments.

The identified opportunities are to build strong relationship with the project sponsor and to deliver a high-quality product baseline.

The threats that have been identified are lowered business priorities, insufficient funding and lack of alignment with external teams.

With this kind of analysis, the project team can now prepare to focus on its' weaknesses and opportunities and highlight its strengths to minimize the external risks or threats.

Similarly, let's look at another sample SWOT done for an organization who wants to increase its revenue share in the market (see Fig. 12).

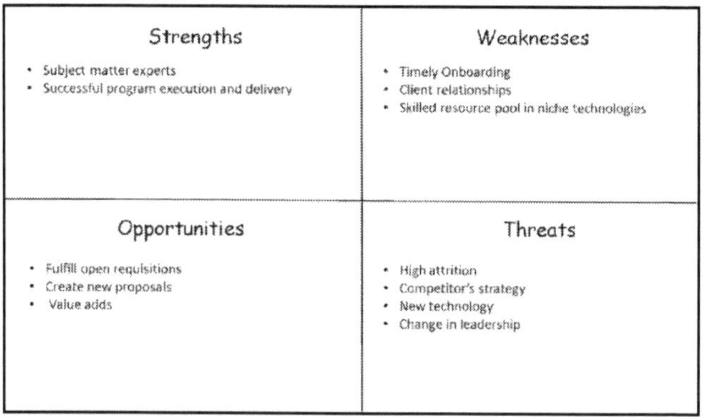

Fig. 12: Sample SWOT for an organization

In the above example, the core strength of this organization is its' people as they are the subject matter experts. Moreover, the organization has a very positive image due to successful execution and implementation of large programs and projects in the past.

The core weaknesses of this sample organization are timely onboarding for open positions, lack of a pool of skilled people who have experience in niche technologies, and lack of strong client relationships.

The opportunities to increase revenue growth are fulfilling open requisitions along with creating new proposals and value adds for their clients.

The core threats are high attrition rate, its' competitor strategy, adoption of new technology, and change in leadership.

With SWOT analysis, an organization can clearly understand its' strengths, weaknesses, opportunities and threats and can take appropriate action to capitalize its' strengths and opportunities, minimize its' weaknesses and be better prepared for any threats.

Chapter 8 – What Is FMEA Technique?

"By failing to prepare, you are preparing to fail."

- *Benjamin Franklin*

FMEA stands for "Failure Modes Effects Analysis". The term "Failure" refers to the defects or problems which can cause negative impact on the consumer of a product, process or a service. The term "Failure Modes" mean the different ways or modes in which something might fail, whereas the term "Effects Analysis" means the study of the consequences of these failures.

Failure modes and effects analysis (FMEA) is a step by step procedure to identify all possible failures in a product, process or a service. This method also enables us to identify the consequences of these failures on the system, process, product, service or the consumer.

In this method, we prioritize or rank the failures per their severity, likelihood of occurrence, and ease of detection ratings. The objective of this method is to identify the highest priority failures.

It was developed in late 1950s to analyze problems of military systems. The automotive industry started to use FMEA by mid 1970s. This methodology is now extensively used in a variety of industries including software and healthcare.

This technique helps to improve the quality and reliability of any product or service. It focusses on early detection of potential failures and hence minimizes the cost of poor quality.

Types of FMEA:

There are many different types of FMEA techniques, depending on what is being analyzed. However, the steps or procedure to conduct an FMEA remains the same. Some widely known FMEA types are as below:

- Concept FMEA
- Design FMEA
- Process FMEA

Concept FMEA (CFMEA):

The Concept FMEA is used to analyze the concepts or the different approaches to build a product. This is usually common during the early stages of product development and is also referred to as 'feasibility study'. It focusses on the identifying and analyzing all potential failure modes in a proposed approach or conceptual design.

Design FMEA (DFMEA):

The Design FMEA is used to analyze the potential problems in a new or an existing design of a product (whether hardware or software) at a system, sub-system or a component level.

Process FMEA (PFMEA):

The Process FMEA is used to analyze the potential problems in any process to improve the same. For example, if an organization wants to systematically analyze all the failure modes for an online payment process, it will use the Process FMEA technique.

Other types of FMEA include Functional FMEA, System FMEA, Service FMEA, and Software FMEA based on what is being analyzed at the time.

How to conduct a FMEA?

There are many steps to conduct FMEA. Here is the detailed procedure for conducting an effective FMEA:

- At first, it is important to assemble a cross functional team of people across departments or knowledge areas such as user interface design, development, testing, product management, sales, product maintenance, customer service etc.

- Then, gather all the available artifacts such as known assumptions, risks, and dependencies along with flowcharts or process diagrams for the systems or sub-systems that are in-scope of this exercise.

- Display the FMEA template to all participants always, and identify all the different features of the system or the sub-system that you are analyzing. The FMEA template is a table created in an excel spreadsheet or drawn on a white board, like the one shown in Fig. 13:

Feature	Potential Failure Mode	Potential Effect(s) of Failure	Severity (S)	Potential Cause(s) of Failure	Occurrence (O)

Current Controls	Detection (D)	RPN	Recommended Action(s)	Assigned To	Due Date

Action Results				
Action Taken	Revised S	Revised O	Revised D	Revised RPN

Fig. 13: FMEA Template

- Identify all the different ways in which a feature or a function may fail. These are the potential failure modes that will then be listed against the feature on the table. To gather thoughts and identify failure modes, you may leverage the technique of brainstorming, which is nothing but a structured way to generate ideas in a group.

- List the potential effects of failure against each failure mode. These are the consequences or the negative impact that the failure may have on the product, system, sub-system, customer, security, performance, dependent systems or services, databases, or compliance regulations.

- You will then write the severity of the effect of failure against each failure mode. This is usually donated by (S), and is rated on a scale of 1-10, where 1 is not severe and 10 is most severe.

- You will then identify all the possible causes of failures for each failure mode. Here, you can leverage the Fishbone method that we learnt earlier in this book. You will then list the most critical causes against the failure mode.

- Next, for each cause, you identify the likelihood of occurrence. This is represented by (O), and is rated on a scale of 1 to 10; where 1 represents extremely unlikely to occur and 10 represents certain to occur or inevitable.

This rating denotes the probability of failure to occur due to the specific cause.

- Again, for each cause, you list down the existing process controls that you have in place. These controls today prevent the cause to occur, reduce the probability of occurrence for the cause or reduce the severity of the failure due to the specific cause.

- You will then list the detection rating for each process control, which means how well the control can detect the failure or cause. This is represented by (D), and is usually rated on a scale of 1 to 10, where 1 is that control will certainly detect the problem or cause and 10 is that control cannot detect the problem or cause at all. This rating helps us to know how well a problem can be detected before it can negatively impact a customer or an end user.

- RPN or the Risk Priority Number is calculated by multiplying the severity (S), occurrence (O) and detection (D) ratings.

RPN denotes the priority in which the failure modes need to be actioned.

- Next column on the table is the recommended action that represents the specific tasks that need to be performed to eliminate the critical causes of each failure mode, to reduce the severity of the problem, to lower the occurrence of the cause or problem or to improve the detection ratings.

- Then, you identify the person to whom the recommended action has been assigned to. This column lists the name of the person who is responsible to act.

- The next column is the due date, which is the date by when the recommended action should take place.

- Next to due date are columns that track the actions being taken and the revised ratings for S, O, and D, along with the revised RPN.

- When the revised RPN is low, you will prioritize other failure modes with higher RPN scores to act.

Chapter 9 - FMEA Examples

"The best way to escape from a problem is to solve it."
- Alan Saporta

Let us consider a web application where customer has the capability to make an online payment by either choosing a one-time payment method or by enrolling his/her debit card into an autopay feature. The application also allows the customer to select his or her statement delivery preference such that the customer can either opt to receive paper statements via postal mail or opt to view online statements on the website. We will now perform a sample FMEA on these features so that the team can focus on highest risk items first.

The below table depicts a sample FMEA analysis conducted for the specified application.

Function	Potential Failure Mode	Potential Effects of Failure	Severity (S)	Potential Cause(s) of Failure	Occurrence (O)	Current Controls	Detection (D)	RPN	Recommended Action(s)	Assign To	Due Date	Action Results				
												Action Taken	Revised S	Revised O	Revised D	Revised RPN
Online Payment	Immediate Payment not working	Loss of business	10	Service Failure	5	Service Monitoring	9	450	Work with the service team to resolve the issue	Product Team	9/30/2016	Deployed the fix	4	2	10	80
	Autopay not working	Customer dis-satisfaction	8	Application Defect	7	Application Logs	6	336	Analyze and fix the application defect	Product Team	9/23/2016	Deployed the fix	4	5	8	160
Enroll in paperless statements	Customer not able to select his statement delivery preference	Customer dis-satisfaction	8	Application Defect	7	Application Logs	8	448	Reproduce the issue and analyze the root cause	Product Team	9/28/2016	Tested the fix	5	4	9	180
	Customer received paper statement when he opted for online statement	Loss of business Customer dis-satisfaction	10	Database Failure	3	Database Logs	3	90	Investigate how many customers are impacted	Product Team	9/30/2016	Identified the fix	8	4	6	192
	Customer received paperless or online statement when opted for paper statements	Customer dis-satisfaction	9	Service Failure	4	Service Monitoring	2	72	Investigate how many customers are impacted	Product Team	9/30/2016	Identified the fix	8	4	4	128

Fig. 14: FMEA Example

Here is the above FMEA example in closer view:

Feature	Potential Failure Mode	Potential Effect(s) of Failure	Severity (S)	Potential Cause(s) of Failure	Occurrence (O)	Current Controls	Detection (D)	RPN
Online Payment	Immediate Payment not working	Loss of business	10	Service Failure	5	Service Monitoring	9	450
	Autopay not working	Customer dis-satisfaction	8	Application Defect	7	Application Logs	6	336
Enroll in paperless statements	Customer not able to select his statement delivery preference	Customer dis-satisfaction	8	Application Defect	7	Application Logs	8	448
	Customer received paper statement when he opted for online statement	Loss to business Customer dis-satisfaction	10	Database Failure	2	Database Logs	4	80
	Customer received paperless or online statement when opted for paper statement	Customer dis-satisfaction	9	Service Failure	4	Service Monitoring	2	72

Recommended Action(s)	Assigned To	Due Date	Action Results				
			Action Taken	Revised S	Revised O	Revised D	Revised RPN
Work with the service team to resolve the issue	Product Team	9/30/2016	Deployed the fix	4	2	10	80
Analyze and fix the application defect	Product Team	9/23/2016	Deployed the fix	4	5	8	160
Reproduce the issue and analyze the root cause	Product Team	9/23/2016	Tested the fix	5	4	9	180
Investigate how many customers are impacted	Product Team	9/30/2016	Identified the fix	8	4	6	192
Investigate how many customers are impacted	Product Team	9/30/2016	Identified the fix	8	4	4	128

In the above example, the team determines the RPN for each potential failure mode, and then takes corrective action for the failures with higher RPN first.

The two failure modes, 'Immediate Payment not working' and 'Customer not able to select his statement delivery preference' have the highest RPN (Risk Priority Number), which means that they have a high severity and can cause highest possible negative customer impact.

They also have high occurrence and detection ratings which means that these failures are most likely to occur but the system does not have a way to detect their occurrence.

With this analysis, the team understands the priority order in which multiple failures need to be addressed.

Likewise, FMEA analysis can be performed for any system or sub-system to identify all the failure modes and their associated consequences. FMEA analysis helps us to focus on the highest risk causes or problems first.

Chapter 10 – What Is 5Whys Technique?

"The problem isn't a shortage of opportunities; it's a lack of perspective."
- *Tim Fargo*

Young kids ask 'Why?' all the time. But who knew that this simple question can help you to drill down to the root of a problem!

5 Whys is the most simple but powerful technique to uncover the root of a problem. The name is 5Whys as '5' is the general rule of thumb for the number of times you need to ask 'Why?' to peel the symptoms and discover the root of a problem.

Sometimes, it may take fewer or more Whys to discover the root cause. This technique does not need any statistical analysis.

Steps to conduct 5Whys:

- First, write the problem on a piece of paper, or on a sticky note.
- Ask the question "Why"
- Write the answer below the question on a separate sticky note
- Ask everyone if this is the root cause of the problem
- Repeat the steps 2-3, until everyone aligns that the root cause of the problem is found.
- Take corrective action for the root cause
- Measure effectiveness of the corrective action. If not effective, then the correct root cause may not have been identified.
- Implement new process or procedure such that the same problem does not repeat.

This technique can be used in any situation, whether it is a personal problem or something at work. It is most commonly used for simple to moderate problems. Sometimes this is the first approach to problem solving, before other complex techniques like Fishbone Diagram or FMEA are explored.

Benefits of 5Whys:

- Simple to understand
- Quick approach to problem solving
- Can be used by individuals or teams

Limitations of 5Whys:

- Participants do not think deeply before identifying root causes or responding to 'Why?'
- There may be difference in opinion when using this technique. People may have different answers to the 'Why?' questions.

Chapter 11 – 5Whys Examples

"Expect problems and eat them for breakfast."

- *Alfred A. Montapert*

In this chapter, we will use 5Whys technique to find the root cause of some sample problems.

Problem: Customers are not able to pay their bills online.

Next, we ask the question 'Why?' and note the result.

Answer: 'Online application is not working as expected'.

Again, the question is 'Why?'

Answer: The production deployment of latest changes introduced a defect in the application.

Again, the question is 'Why?'

Answer: Regression testing was not done

Again, the question is 'Why?'

Answer: Test accounts were not working

Again, the question is 'Why?'

Answer: Lack of time to secure working test accounts.

Here, in this example, the team aligns that the root cause for this problem is lack of time. The team then takes the corrective action for their next release and plans the additional time necessary to ensure that the test accounts are in a good condition and that the regression testing gets completed prior to any code deployment.

Now, let's look at another application of 5Whys technique as below:

Problem: My boss is not happy with me ☹

Question: Why?

Answer: I did not complete the work assigned to me!

Question: Why?

Answer: I don't have the required knowledge on the new tools and technologies being used in the project.

Question: Why?

Answer: I did not spend any time to learn the same.

Question: Why?

Answer: I did not prioritize the training over other tasks.

In this example, the root cause for an unhappy boss is the lack of commitment by the individual to spend time and learn new technology.

Likewise, you can use 5Whys technique to peel off the layers and find the real root cause of a problem.

Chapter 12 – Comparison

"The only person who is educated is the one who has learned how to learn and change."

- *Carl Rogers*

In this chapter, you will learn which problem solving technique will work best for you. So far, you have learnt about five widely used problem solving techniques – Fishbone, Brainstorming, SWOT, FMEA and 5Whys. We will now discuss the different problems or situations and the technique that will work best in that situation.

Typically, when you want to gather feedback or seek comments (not necessarily trying to solve a problem), the technique that is well suited is brainstorming. On the other hand, if you have multiple problems and you want to decide which one to prioritize, FMEA will work best for you.

Again, if you want to perform a health check or assess an organization, program, project or individual, the best technique is SWOT analysis. SWOT analysis can be done at any time irrespective of any problem.

If your primary objective is to understand and rank the multiple root causes to a complex problem, then fishbone analysis is the best choice. However, if all you need is to find the root cause to a simple to moderate problem, 5Whys technique might work best for you.

If you have a well-defined problem, then either 5Whys, Brainstorming or Fishbone analysis may work for you. Most often, one likes to conduct a self-analysis by leveraging either of these three techniques, before conducting a formal analysis with his team, peers, friends or family members.

Brainstorming and fishbone analysis work hand in hand with each other. Some teams conduct brainstorming session prior to conducting a fishbone diagram. The ideas that are generated during the brainstorming session are then leveraged and categorized during fishbone analysis.

While brainstorming technique encourages the group to generate as many ideas as possible, fishbone diagram provides a structure to the thoughts in the form of categories, and enables a ranking of the identified causes.

The below diagram provides a quick snapshot of the comparison between the different problem solving techniques covered in this book.

Fishbone	Brainstorming	SWOT	FMEA	5Whys
Most effective when conducted in a group	Most effective when conducted in a group	Most effective when conducted in a group	Most effective when conducted in a group	Effective when conducted either individually or in a group
Highly effective when problem is well defined	Can also be used to gather feedback and comments	Can be conducted anytime with or without a problem	Highly effective when multiple problems exist that are well defined	Highly effective when a problem is simple to moderate and is well defined
Identifies all the possible root causes to a problem	Works hand in hand with Fishbone analysis	Identifies the weaknesses and threats for an entity or an individual	Identifies all the failure modes and impact of a problem	Identifies the real cause to a problem
Provides structure to thoughts and enables ranking of causes	Generates as many ideas as possible	Defines strengths, weaknesses, oppurtunities and threats	Calculates the risk priority number to help prioritize the risks or failure modes	Used to peel off the layers and find the real cause of the problem
Highly effective when tackling one problem at a time	Highly effective when tackling one problem at a time	Highly effective when performed for a single entity (organization, program, project or individual)	Highly effective when tackling more than one problem at a time as it helps to prioritize the actions	Highly effective when tackling one problem at a time

Fig. 15: Comparison of problem solving tools

Now that you have learnt the key problem solving techniques, think about applying these techniques to some of your problems today. The more you apply these techniques, the more comfortable you will get with these. With this, I sincerely hope that you find an effective solution to all your problems!

Bibliography

Wikipedia. (2016). Ishikawa diagram. Retrieved Sept 2016 from Wikipedia: https://en.wikipedia.org/wiki/Ishikawa_diagram

Wikipedia. (2016). Brainstorming. Retrieved Sept 2016 from Wikipedia: https://en.wikipedia.org/wiki/Brainstorming

The Mind Tools Editorial Team. SWOT Analysis. https://www.mindtools.com/

Van Vliet, V. (2010). SWOT Analysis. Retrieved Sept 2016 from ToolsHero: http://www.toolshero.com/problem-solving/swot-analysis

23405352R00047

Printed in Great Britain
by Amazon